PRACTICAL MEDITATION
FOR BEGINNERS

A 5-Step Guide to Regaining Balance, Mindfulness and Better Sleep

The Best 7 Techniques to Learn How to Calm the Mind,
Reduce Stress and Improve Concentration

Mind Change Academy

Mind Change Academy © Copyright 2022 - All rights reserved.

The content contained within this book may not be reproduced, duplicated or transmitted without direct written permission from the author or the publisher.

Under no circumstances will any blame or legal responsibility be held against the publisher, or author, for any damages, reparation, or monetary loss due to the information contained within this book. Either directly or indirectly.

Legal Notice:

This book is copyright protected. This book is only for personal use. You cannot amend, distribute, sell, use, quote or paraphrase any part, or the content within this book, without the consent of the author or publisher.

Disclaimer Notice:

Please note the information contained within this document is for educational and entertainment purposes only. All effort has been executed to present accurate, up to date, and reliable, complete information. No warranties of any kind are declared or implied. Readers acknowledge that the author is not engaging in the rendering of legal, financial, medical or professional advice. The content within this book has been derived from various sources. Please consult a licensed professional before attempting any techniques outlined in this book.

By reading this document, the reader agrees that under no circumstances is the author responsible for any losses, direct or indirect, which are incurred as a result of the use of the information contained within this document, including, but not limited to, — errors, omissions, or inaccuracies.

Your Free Gift

As a way of saying thanks for your purchase, I'm offering a free report that's exclusive to readers of this book.

With EMOTIONAL DIARY you'll discover a printable reference journal of rules to know how to manage your emotions.

Writing all the emotions you feel is the first step to see their effect on your life, to understand them and finally manage them to live a more peaceful life.

Everything you need to get started with EMOTIONAL DIARY is to download your free diary.

Click this link to free download
https://dl.bookfunnel.com/qx1qtousl6

Meditation Music

We have created a YouTube channel to give you the opportunity to listen to relaxing music to meditate, relax, study, work and sleep better.

The numerous beneficial effects of music on the human being have been confirmed by many scientific researches around the world. Listening to it increases the production of serotonin (a natural antidepressant), reduces the secretion of stress hormones (cortisol) and stimulates the production of beta-endorphins (analgesics produced by the body), acting as a real antidote against states of anxiety, insomnia and psychophysical fatigue.

Meditation music, for example, is a very effective tool for combating stress, easing tensions, alleviating the rhythms of modern life and bringing general well-being.

It also has a positive effect on feelings of depression, anxiety or loneliness, but a close relationship between music, cognitive processes and human mood has also been demonstrated.

These are just some of the benefits you can gain from listening to relaxing music for meditation:
- Relief from stress and anxiety
- Improves the quality of rest and sleep by calming the nerves and diverting attention from a noisy brain.
- Increases concentration and memory capacity
- Improves physical health by helping your body heal and rest
- Rebalances heart and respiratory function
- Reduces blood pressure levels
- Improves blood oxygenation through deep breathing
- Activates energy and vitality levels
- Helps with positive thinking

- Increases self-awareness
- Stimulates creativity
- Instils self-esteem

Practical Meditation For Beginners — Mind Change Academy

Discover the best products for Meditating

If you are new to the world of meditation, now is the right time to gear up and get off on the right foot.

Meditation accessories, if well chosen, can help you create your own space to devote yourself to this wellness practice more effectively.

And remember that, according to some studies, it only takes 10 minutes of meditation a day to experience the first benefits in daily life.

Download our free PDF https://BookHip.com/VCTKVKN and.........

Good meditation……

Table of Contents

INTRODUCTION 10

CHAPTER 1: WHAT IS MEANT BY MEDITATION AND MINDFULNESS 14

    WHAT IS MEDITATION? 15
    MINDFULNESS 20

CHAPTER 2: THE HISTORY AND BENEFITS OF MEDITATION 26

    THE HISTORY OF MEDITATION 27
    THE BENEFITS OF MEDITATION 28
    THE FRUITS OF PRACTICING MEDITATION 31

CHAPTER 3: HOW AND WHY MEDITATING WILL IMPROVE YOUR LIFE 34

    HOW AND WHEN TO START AND PRACTICAL ADVICE 37

CHAPTER 4. HOW TO PREPARE FOR MEDITATION 41

CHAPTER 5: THE 5 STEPS TO PROPER MEDITATION 48

    BE COMFORTABLE 49
    POSTURE 51
    ATTENTION 52
    BREATH 53
    THOUGHTS 54

CHAPTER 6: TYPES OF MEDITATION 56

    AUDITORY MEDITATION 57
    BODY SCAN MEDITATION 58
    MEDITATION FOR A GOOD NIGHT'S SLEEP 60

CHAPTER 7: THE 7 MOST EFFECTIVE MEDITATION TECHNIQUES 74

    MINDFULNESS MEDITATION (VIPASSANA) 75

- Walking meditation 81
- Zen meditation 87
- Transcendental Meditation 93
- Dynamic Meditation 98
- Yoga meditation 102
- Ho'oponopono meditation 110

CONCLUSION **115**

Introduction

Meditation is a type of practice that deals with calming your mind and clearing it of thoughts. When you do this, you can start to become truly still and experience the natural state of peace in between thoughts. Meditation consists of various types of meditation and many ways to practice it. One way of practicing meditation is using mindfulness, which is the notion that "your present experience is your best teacher." When you do this, you avoid judging yourself or others during an encounter and instead give yourself a better chance of connecting with your true self. With such a broad range of benefits to consider, there is no excuse not to meditate.

In the modern world, our minds are filled with worries and anxieties that can often plague us during our day-to-day routines. Meditation allows you to step away from these thoughts for a time and instead focus on your current state.

Meditation has many different benefits, but one of the most important ones is stress relief. The autonomic stress response is a response to real or perceived threats that cause an increase in blood pressure and heart rate, an angry or fearful mental state, alertness in the presence of danger and rapid muscular response.

The choice of meditation you choose to practice will depend on a number of factors.

For example, Buddhist Meditation focuses on mindfulness, which is the notion that "your present experience is your best teacher." Mindfulness is a key concept in Buddhism, but it can also be used in many different contexts and ways. Some advantages gained from the practice include a sense of calmness, improved emotional regulation and reduced anxiety.

Another type of meditation is Insight meditation and it is said to be one of the most important forms of meditation. "Insight" can be defined as a sudden opening up to the truth about oneself and others, a sharpening of one's mind, a deeper understanding of what it means to be human, or simply the ability to see things as they are without bias or judgment.

Meditation has been the focus of many studies over the years. It can also help lower stress and anxiety levels, help with blood pressure, and improve sleep quality. However, it's also important to note that meditation doesn't just work on your body.

Researchers note that meditation increases the Gamma Wave Frequency range of the brain, which is associated with increased focus, creativity, and overall consciousness. In other words, it improves your ability to think more clearly.

Also known as "brainwave entrainment," meditation can help entrain your brainwaves to various frequencies and produce various effects.

Meditation has been scientifically proven to benefit not only your physical well-being but also help you improve mental peace and happiness. Meditation is more than just a hobby--it's science.

The benefits of meditation have been recognized for years, but now more and more people realize their potential benefits. What once was a different practice is now a dynamic way to change your life.

Chapter 1: What is meant by Meditation and Mindfulness

What is Meditation?

Meditation acts as a mental exercise that helps us to remain calm and thinks clearly.

In today's world, there is stress and strain everywhere. Be it in a relationship or at your job; stress is unavoidable. Modern gadgets and our minute-to-minute lifestyle add to our stress factor majorly. People are looking for ways to relax and release their stress. That is why we see gyms and yoga studios up and about in every corner of the world. But no gym is good enough; your gym might help you to lose some weight and look glamorous, but running on the treadmill in an air-conditioned room alone does not provide one with a calm and tranquil mind. Working out your mind is much more important than pulling a few muscles. Freeing the mind from droning thoughts and everyday training is the main aim of meditation.

Man is a social animal and though we are at peace with ourselves for the first few years of our life, our daily interactions result in a worked-up mess as we grow old. It is then that complaints, confusions and worries become second nature to us. And that is when we feel at a loss of harmony. I would like to assure you that peace has to be found from within and not from the outside world. The outside world has and shall never provide the serenity you wish for. It's from within that serenity must be found. Sit in a quiet place and look within yourself. When your senses are in a state of silence, you'll feel real peace.

Your mind is like a monkey. It flits from one craving to another, trying to engorge the senses with the pleasures of the instant. When the mind is filled with distractions, how can it concentrate on one goal? The solution is to control the senses with the power of your mind. It is here that meditation helps. Sitting in a place for at least ten minutes a day concentrating on a single object can also help you to keep calm and concentrate on a specific goal. Peace and tranquility are part and parcel of our mental makeup. It is there with us every single moment of our life. Only we don't recognize it. That is because we're ignorant about the calm when all along it is there right within us. We're so caught up with the external world that we forget to look within to find tranquility.

Being at peace with yourself is what matters and meditation helps you to achieve exactly that. Meditation has proved to be the best alternative therapy. Even doctors around the world recommend their patients perform meditation to be free from worries.

You need two things to achieve freedom from stress and worry. A silent mind and an open heart!

Popular misconceptions about meditation

There is a popular misconception that meditation is a part of the Hindu religion. Because of it, many people have lost a huge opportunity to derive benefits from this practice. I am saying it here once again for clarification – Meditation has nothing to do even remotely with any religion. By meditating, you will not become a heathen. You can practice meditation even when following your religion. Meditation does not discriminate between Christians, Muslims, Jews or any other form of religion. Perhaps the beauty of meditation lies in the fact that anyone and everyone can practice it without compromising their religious beliefs.

The second misconception which keeps people away from meditation is that it's very tough and difficult. I have heard stories that claim that mediation means sitting in one posture for hours together. Another popular myth is that meditation means abstaining from the pleasures of life. There are absurd claims that meditation requires you to be celibate - not to have sex. Who would want to take up meditation if there are so many restrictions on practicing it?

Let me put the above misconceptions to rest. You don't have to do it for hours in meditation. At the very most, you may have to be still for thirty minutes. Meditation is not hard work or manual labor. There are no restrictions on having sex or enjoying the good life. It actually empowers you to enjoy life to the fullest. It enables you to be active, energetic and joyful. You are all fired up and ready to go after a session of mediation. Sometimes, meditation is compared to having drugs without the side effects. Practitioners of meditation have confessed to a greater level of awareness and a sense of everlasting happiness. It brings perspective to life and creates opportunities at a subconscious level.

Meditation is sometimes wrongly compared to black magic. I don't know where or how this concept originated, but I can tell you that it's utter rubbish. Meditation has nothing to do with magic – black, white or any other color.

I have mentioned many times that meditation is a spiritual practice. This may seem confusing to many readers. By spirituality, I mean that mediation is a practice to reach a greater level of consciousness. This consciousness is universal and an inherent part of the human condition regardless of their religion. Pure consciousness refers to a true understanding of our life. It's also called realization. Words life awareness, insight, and vision are related to the concept of consciousness.

Now that you know about the facts of meditation, you can confidently embrace it and enjoy its true benefits.

Meditation is a way of life

Your body consists of flesh, blood and the nervous system. Each part of your body must be in harmony if you want to achieve happiness and wellbeing. Meditation helps in reaching a state of well-being in which you are completely relaxed and find joy. There are a lot of reasons why people practice meditation. Some take up meditation for relief from a temporary problem. There are people who want to discover their inner selves. Spirituality is another goal that people pursue using meditation as a tool. You must have noticed that people have become health conscious. You can only have a healthy body if you have a healthy mind. Health problems are generally related to stress and worries. Meditation is a fantastic way to get rid of tension.

Meditation has been proved to heal mental diseases as well. Mediation can work wonders for patients suffering from mental disorders if accompanied by suitable medication. You should not take medicines without consulting a physician. Many people may not be diagnosed with serious mental sickness but yet may suffer its debilitating effect. Many cases go unnoticed and undiagnosed. Meditation can be effective in avoiding the escalation of mental illness.

Interestingly many physical ailments are related to our mind. It is scientifically proven that cardiac failures can occur because of sudden stress. Chronic headaches, belly aches and muscular pain are associated with the mental state. In such cases, meditation is a viable solution. By de-stressing the mind and allowing free flow of energy, you can control, if not totally eliminate, physical distress. Meditation must become a way of life and daily practice.

Essentially, meditation is a practice that helps to keep the mind still and stay calm. You can learn these techniques within a few minutes. Sit erect in a place and close your eyes. Try to concentrate on one single object or nothing. There ……. Now you have started your meditating session.

Mindfulness

Mindfulness is a presence at the moment. That may sound obvious or even obtuse, but when you begin to think about what you ponder and where your thoughts tend to go most of the time, you'll begin to realize why we are rarely mindful of the present moments in our lives.

What were you just thinking when you started to read this book? Did you think about all of the times that you didn't feel at peace? Did you wish that you could be more comfortable with yourself, with your situation in life, with the amount of money that you had, the kind of education that you received, or anything else?

Did you think about someone you met recently? Or about someone you lost?

Were you pondering the next purchase that you will make, such as having to go grocery shopping this evening or the TV that you saw in the store the other day?

You see, all around us, at every moment, there are plenty of things to distract us from the here and now. It doesn't mean that we can't be thinking about those things, but for the majority of people in today's world, it tends to consume their lives, and they might focus on the bad things that happened in their life or the regrets that they have.

When you sit back and truly think about it, you might begin to realize that you're in a lot of pain. Emotional pain, physical pain, spiritual pain … no matter what type of pain it is, it's real and it can keep you from fulfilling your life's promise.

It doesn't have to continue to be that way, though. Being mindful of the present, of what you have, the pain that you are experiencing, the suffering that you endure, and the dreams and hopes that you have ... can help you find more peace within your life.

It can help you discover what you *truly* want in life rather than what you *think* you should want.

Why do you think you know what you want

We have free will. No matter what you want to do, you can do it. If that means working 80 hours a week for 40 years so that you can afford a life of luxury, then you can do that. If you want to go out and commit a crime, you're free to do so, although you also need to be willing to pay the price for your actions.

If you want to ask someone out on a date, there is no one stopping you. You might believe that because the person's mother or father told you that you couldn't date their daughter or their son, you can't ask, but you *can*. You see, you have free will.

As a result, you can choose to do anything you want. While you're growing up, while you're going to school, and even while you're working, you do these things because you have to, because you want to, and then because you want certain things out of life.

If you wanted to just sit back and not do anything in your life if you wanted to be lazy and live in your parent's basement still when you're in your forties because they allow you to, then that might be fine for some people, but for the majority of us, there are things that we want in life.

The nice house.

The loving spouse.

Children.

A house.

A nice car.

To take vacations.

After a while, the list of basic wants and needs begins to change and you might be focused on 'keeping up with the Joneses,' so to speak. This means that you begin to accumulate friends and you want the same things that they want, or you want *better* than they have.

If your best friend or cousin or someone else you know buys a five-bedroom house on a lake, you focus on getting a *six*-bedroom house with an incredible view. If your neighbor goes out and buys a 25-foot boat to take out on the weekends, you plan to buy a 28-footer.

If your sister ends up living in a better neighborhood than you, then you might plan on getting out of your neighborhood.

This is often driven by insecurity and a feeling of emptiness. When you don't feel complete, then you're constantly going to be chasing other things in the hope that you *will* feel complete one day.

So you end up chasing what other people have because you believe that they are happy and you want that same level of happiness.

But the larger house with the nice view will only provide an illusion of happiness for a while until someone else seems to get something better.

The better neighborhood doesn't have the same vibe or atmosphere that you enjoyed in the previous location.

That boat just sits there after the first year because you don't seem to have the time to enjoy it because you're working overtime just to keep up with all of the bills.

It's enough to drive any sane person crazy. And it's *all* keeping you from being *mindful* of what you do have at the moment. And it's keeping you from having peace and contentment.

The marketing magic

Back about 60 years ago, shortly after World War II came to an end, the country as a whole was working on trying to recover and heal from all of the pain that the war brought. Even though the majority of the country had been safe from direct harm, millions of men were injured or died during the war and that left a lot of emotional scars to heal.

The country was finally pulling itself out of the tail remnants of the Great Depression, but people didn't have a lot of disposable income. Washing machines, television sets, and other appliances were fairly new to most homes and because money was still tight, the majority of homeowners and homemakers couldn't justify spending the kind of money that it cost for these items.

So manufacturers of these items decided that the only way to sell their high-ticket items was to create the need for them. They focused on marketing and advertising, spreading the image of happy people using these products, generating the notion that if you purchased this item, you were going to be happy, fulfilled, and complete, too.

It worked wonders. Sales for items that had once been considered luxury items began to soar and the marketing age was born.

Today, everywhere you turn, it's one more marketing package trying to convince you that you'll be better off with this item or that one and now the majority of us tend to fall for those ideas.

These marketing campaigns take us out of the moment, and convince us to *imagine our lives* being better if we *only had this one item*. So you get hooked on that idea and drawn out of the present moment.

You're drawn away from mindfulness.

You're drawn away from the emotions, feelings, and experiences that you have every second of every day. You may feel depressed, sad, lonely, unfulfilled, empty, hollow, or a host of other emotions and continue to focus on external factors.

These external factors could be those aforementioned items that you believe will bring you joy and happiness, ease the pain, or make you feel better. They could be incidents that you blame for what you're going through.

If you can't be mindful of the present moment, if you can't work through the things that you're dealing with right now, *you will never truly find peace* because you will constantly be searching for something to fill the void that you feel.

Being mindful of your present state, your present state of consciousness is one of the keys to finding peace within yourself.

Chapter 2: The History and Benefits of Meditation

The History of Meditation

Meditation was barely recognized by Westerners until an Indian yoga teacher named Maharishi Mahesh Yogi introduced Transcendental Meditation (TM) to the United States in 1959. The meditation presented by Maharishi to Americans used a mantra that helped to stimulate relaxation and transcend conventional thinking.

The Beatles, who studied with Maharishi in India, were a big influence on the growing popularity of meditation through the 1960s. With his popularity, Maharishi continued to train more than forty thousand meditation teachers for the next fifty years. The teachers who trained directly under Maharishi then spread out and taught the Transcendental Meditation technique to more than five million people around the world.

During the last part of the 20th century, other methods of meditation began to gain recognition in the West. One of these new forms of meditation was called insight or mindfulness meditation.

Mindfulness meditation aims to help a person become deeply aware of the present moment in order to be able to completely live through the here and now.

Other forms of meditation utilize visualization and guided imagery through mental pictures to promote relaxation of both mind and body. Currently, over 20 million Americans, which comprise almost 10% of the population, perform regular meditation.

Their purpose for practicing meditation ranges from managing high blood pressure, stress, anxiety, and their overall state of mind in order to live better.

The Benefits of Meditation

As meditation increased in popularity over the years, more and more studies were conducted to explore the effects meditation has on the human mind and body. Scientists extensively researched the potential benefits of meditation and how it could help cure a wide range of physical, mental, emotional, and even societal ailments.

Since its introduction in 1959, more than 600 research studies on meditation have been carried out at 250 different universities and medical schools around the world to confirm the effectiveness of meditation.

The National Institutes of Health in the United States granted more than $24 million for research studies on the topic of meditation. These research studies are now recorded in more than 650 scientific and medical journals, each of which provides proof of the benefits of meditation for medical conditions such as diabetes, cancer, chronic pain, and heart disease.

Because of the deemed benefits of meditation, many businesses have started sponsoring meditation classes for their employees' well-being. This cost-effective solution enhances employee productivity and keeps them happy.

Even public schools in the United States have started to teach meditation to both children and teenagers. A research study conducted by the Medical College of Georgia in 2003 discovered that meditation lowers stress and enhances interpersonal relationships between students. It was also discovered that it improves school performance.

The government has also started using meditation to lower crime rates, and the US military uses meditation as an effective treatment for post-traumatic stress disorder acquired by soldiers sent out to war.

The Primary Benefits of Meditation

Meditation has been basically practiced in the East for several centuries though it is fairly new to the western world. Its benefits and ease of implementation have been recognized by a western culture which has led to its rapid popularity growth.

For just a few minutes a day, with absolutely no cost or special equipment, anyone can take advantage of the benefits of meditation.

Despite its simplicity, the overall efficacy of meditation has made it the most valuable means for people to heal not themselves alone but the planet as well.

A summary of the primary benefits of meditation

Benefits for the body

- Reduces inflammation by alleviating stress through relaxation. Stress leads to inflammation. Relaxation turns off the stress response, therefore, reducing the health risks caused by inflammation
- Lowers high blood pressure by making the body less responsive to stress hormones
- Decreases anxiety attacks by lowering the levels of blood lactate
- Boosts the production of serotonin which improves mood and behavior
- Reduces stress-related ailments, including headaches, insomnia, and ulcers

- Boosts the immune system
- Improves energy levels

Benefits for the mind

- Creates emotional strength that helps fight against negative feelings of anger, tension, and frustration
- Improves creative inclinations
- Boosts feelings of happiness
- Helps put things into perspective. Problems that appeared big begin to appear small
- Expands intuition through improved clarity and peace of mind
- Improves focus and concentration
- Promotes calmness by not allowing any single negative thought to dominate the mind or body

The fruits of practicing Meditation

Physical benefits:

- Lowers blood pressure
- Cures insomnia
- Decreases respiratory rate
- Helps to breathe well
- Controls asthma
- Helps to reduce pain due to arthritis
- Aids weight loss
- Good for cardiovascular diseases
- Reduces cholesterol
- Boosts immune system
- Heals headache
- Cures infertility (the block that occurs due to irregular blood flow to the lower part of the body gets removed with chakra meditation)
- Prevents eating disorder

Mental Benefits:

- Gives Inner peace
- Helps you to De-stress
- Makes you happy
- Gives contentment
- Gratitude
- Show Compassion
- Forgiveness
- Healer
- Reduces anxiety
- Cures OCD (obsessive-compulsive disorder)
- Reduces depression
- Mood enhancer

- Improves concentration
- Anger management
- Develop tolerance
- Aids positive thinking
- Silences negative thoughts
- Motivational
- Deal with failures

Spiritual Benefits:

- Helps you to become more intuitive
- Makes you aware of your surroundings
- You transcend into a higher plane of consciousness
- Therapeutic
- Clarity in thought
- Learn to reach your subconscious
- Cultivate inner strength

You'll be surprised at the transformation that you undergo when you under take meditation. Within a week of starting the practice, you'll find yourself composed and busy within yourself. You'll not need long to be with people. You'll prefer your own private moments where you can tune in and get in touch with your inner self.

Chapter 3: How and why meditating will improve your life

So what's the point of meditating? Couldn't you achieve more mindfulness just by concentrating on it more? Wouldn't it be just as effective to sit there and make sure that you focus on living in the here and now?

If it were really that easy, then everyone would be more mindful of their present state of mind. Yet the truth is that almost everyone lives in a state that is not the present. Sure, we pay attention to where we're going, and we have work that needs to be done, but this is nothing more than just 'going through the motions.

What about the way you feel in your life? What about the loss that you experienced recently? When a relationship ends or someone close to us passes away, or you lose a job that supports you … these can all cause pain.

Many other things can cause pain as well, and it's true that we tend to remember the bad things that happen to us or the mistakes that we make more than we remember the good things.

After all, most so-called 'good things that happen to us are not something we focus on. You drive through traffic and make it to work on time. That's a good thing, but not something that you focus on.

You paid your mortgage on time for the tenth year in a row. That's a good thing, but you don't see it as such. Miss one payment, pay it late or have an issue and you're going to be thinking about that mistake all the time, right?

Why is this? Why do we give so much energy to these mistakes and negative experiences?

Some would say that it's simply easier to accept mistakes and dwell on them than it is to focus on the small and big successes in life. Walking up the stairs without tripping is a success, but it's an expected one. Trip while walking up the stairs and you'll have that in the back of your mind for a long time.

When you meditate, especially with the goal of achieving more mindfulness, you're going to reach a point when you can live in the moment rather than dwelling on the past, especially the things that went wrong.

If you have ever been really involved in a relationship with someone and things didn't work out the way you had hoped, especially if you thought that things were good and your partner was the one who broke it off, what did you do?

If you're like most people, you might have sat there and tried to determine what went wrong. What did you do that upset them? You may have spent days, even weeks, trying to figure out what you did wrong.

You see, most of us focus on the pain, the suffering in our life as though that's going to teach us something by looking back. The truth is that you can't learn anything new from what has already happened.

Sure, you can analyze a problem and find some solution for the future, but most of the time, we simply keep rehashing the same things over and over until you're no longer paying attention to what's going on in your life right now.

Meditation can help you achieve more mindfulness by giving yourself the focus to live in the moment, let go of the past, embrace the pain and suffering that you've felt, and then finally be able to let it go.

How and When to Start and Practical Advice

There are countless reasons why none of us have time in our schedules to meditate. Although we are all aware of the advantages, we nonetheless struggle with stress and suffering on a daily basis because we have grown accustomed to it and are unable to imagine what life would be like without it. Therefore, the actual query is not, "Why are we not practicing meditation," but rather, "What are we waiting for?" We find time for so many other everyday tasks that don't offer any value to our lives, yet we make up reasons not to complete a straightforward workout that could make our lives so much simpler and more enjoyable.

Spend a few minutes and think about how much time you have spent over the past few days with things like watching television, surfing the internet, texting friends, chatting on the telephone, or maybe just plain stressed out worrying about some life event that you're struggling with. It's a proven fact that meditation can help you focus better and feel less stress, which helps you become more productive when you go about your daily life—whether it's as a CEO of a major company or studying for college classes or anything in between. Why would you not want to invest a few minutes in yourself if you knew that you could improve the remaining hours in your day?

Meditation costs nothing other than your time. You may have seen professional instructors with fancy pillows and pretty costumes teaching classes, but that does not mean you have to invest in those items to start your own meditation program. What you need is a quiet place with no interruptions, a comfortable place to place your bottom on, comfortable clothing so you can breathe with ease, and about ten to twenty minutes.

Meditation can be done in less than twenty minutes or more, depending on you and your lifestyle; however, for the ease of learning, we will discuss beginning in terms of ten to twenty-minute segments, so you actually give yourself a real break from the world around you and allow your body time to adjust to this new skill you are learning to master. Once you have developed a technique that works for you, you will be able to adjust it to meet your needs accordingly.

There is a debate amongst professionals as to when the best time to meditate is and, again, it has to be based on your lifestyle to make it work. However, to begin, it is recommended that you practice this new skill twice a day for maximum benefit right from the start and adjust later when you have developed good skills. With that said, it's best to start with ten to twenty minutes first thing in the morning before you face any of the stresses of the day so you can begin your day on a relaxed note, and then ten to twenty minutes at the end of your day so you can go to bed relaxed and not full of tension from the day you just lived. Yes, that's twenty to forty minutes out of your day, but those will be the best minutes of each day and well worth the effort. If that is just too much to start with, then at least start each day off with a meditation session so you can begin to feel the benefits and gain an understanding of the technique and what works for you.

When you first start, those minutes will seem like hours and you might feel guilty for wasting time. That is human nature and expected, so remind yourself of the health benefits you are seeking to achieve and stick with it. If you miss one of your sessions, do not use it as an excuse to stop; make use of it as an excuse to reevaluate your value to yourself. You are very important and anything you can do to improve your life is something that you should continue to do, especially since it's free, something you get to have control over, and something that you have made the choice to do and not something that is controlled by outsiders. This is your body and your life. Meditation is your chance to improve both.

It is also advised that if at all possible, you practice meditation in a sitting position versus lying down. The real reason for this is that you might become so relaxed that you fall asleep, and you will not have really achieved the true benefit of meditation. However, if for health reasons you are bedridden and cannot sit upright, do not let that stop you from practicing meditation. You may need to modify your technique so that you do not fall asleep in the process; however, meditation will still have the same health benefits no matter what position you are in at the time of utilizing this skill.

Loose clothing is also recommended because it is very hard to concentrate on your breathing or any other body part or external object if you're being pinched or poked by uncomfortable clothing. It does not really matter what you wear as long as you are free to breathe and relax.

Some professionals recommend a timer and others do not. That choice would have to be up to you. Personally, it's easier not to have something ticking away either physically or even mentally reminding us that time is so important that we have to be a slave to it. If at all possible, schedule your meditation time for a time when it does not matter if you go over twenty minutes so that if you feel the need to stay in a meditative state longer, you're free to do so. There is nothing wrong with you having a clock or watch close by that you check to see if twenty minutes have passed; however, there is nothing more jarring to the nerves than to be relaxed and have an alarm go off. It can undo those precious minutes' worth of relaxation in a single heartbeat.

It is never advisable to meditate when you're hungry. Your mind will want to focus on your stomach and little else. If at all possible, have a small snack if you need to meditate on an empty stomach. This will allow you to be more focus on what you need to focus on and not what the body is lacking. The same is true for a full stomach. If you have just eaten, odds are you will fall asleep if you become fully relaxed through the meditative process.

It goes without saying that it will be impossible to meditate if you need to use the restroom. So be sure to take care of this urgent matter just prior to your meditation exercise to ensure that you are not bothered by an urge to "go" five minutes after you start to relax. Sometimes it just happens, is unplanned, and can't be helped, but being aware of this issue prior to starting usually helps in the long run and helps with your comfort level.

Of course, if you ever feel pain or discomfort, please feel free to adjust your posture, your location, your lighting, or whatever it is that interferes with your ability to meditate. Meditation should never cause true physical discomfort to the point of pain. You may experience some discomfort from setting on the ground if you are not familiar with sitting this way, but that will pass after a couple of days. Also, it never hurts to have supporters that can take your children or your pets for a short period of time if they prove to be a distraction that you cannot work around.

It is a good idea to speak with your doctor if you have medical issues to seek advice about what might aid you in your meditative process. Most doctors understand the therapeutic benefits of meditation and will be an encouraging supporters on your journey in this process. And if you are experiencing any kind of physical discomfort, a doctor may be able to advise you about different postures that are more suited to your body's mobility and flexibility range.

Chapter 4. How to Prepare for Meditation

Preparing for meditation is Stage Zero of the meditation process. With any kind of meditation, it is important to do some preparation in order for things to go well.

Stage Zero is often seen as an optional extra and either skipped or not done thoroughly. This is sad because it hinders the effectiveness of one's meditation even before it begins.

If you want to get a certain result, you need to set up the right conditions to get that result. According to Buddhists, there is a principle called "conditionality," which states that if your goal is to achieve "x," you need to set up the conditions that will enable you to achieve "x."

Buddhists put a heavy emphasis on the importance of preparation. They believe that it's impossible to skip this step and expect to get the results that you desire.

Preparing for meditation involves both the external and internal. Externally you want to prepare a place that will be conducive to a deep, meditative experience. Internally, you want to address your posture, deepen your awareness of your body, and relax as deeply as you can. This preparation is essential for a calmer, less stressed and more peaceful mind.

Following are some suggestions on how you can prepare your external and internal environment in a way that will help you get the most out of your meditation.

Mirror your internal intention by an external act

Mentally you are emptying your mind of all irrelevant, powerless human thoughts in order to reload it with thoughts that are in line with your spiritual higher self.

By taking a shower (to wash away your anxieties), brushing your teeth, or washing your hands and face, you can demonstrate physically that you want to purify your thoughts. Self-washing is a highly symbolic cleansing process that will leave you feeling revitalized, clean, and refreshed. As you get ready to meditate, it can also have a very positive impact on your disposition and frame of mind., and an effect on your mood and overall mindset you prepare to meditate.

Create a relaxing atmosphere

If you want your body and mind to relax, then create an atmosphere that is conducive to relaxation.

Light a candle, burn some incense, dim the lights, place some fresh flowers on the table, or play some meditation music. Creating a sanctuary in which to meditate will go a long way in helping you clear your mind and experience a deep, enjoyable and enriching meditation.

Provoke a meditative state

Take 5-20 minutes to read spiritual writings. These can vary between biblical God-centered writings, spiritual healing material, or even some positive, encouraging words that feed your soul and get you in touch with Spirit. As you read, absorb and reflect on the meaning of every sentence. Take notes in a special journal that you exclusively reserve for spiritual reflection.

Breathe deep

When you feel that your spiritual reading has led you to a state of awareness and peace, take between 5-10 slow deep breaths. As you breathe inward, open yourself to the peace-loving nature of God (or Universe). Let your outward breath release the tension and frustrations that are held within your unconscious. Let them go. Now begin the meditation practice of your choice. Breathe from your diaphragm and feel your body relaxing with every full, deep breath.

Choose the best time for you

There is no set of rules in terms of the ideal time to meditate. It will depend on what works best for you and your schedule.

Morning meditation is preferred by some people because it helps set a good mood for the rest of the day. Others prefer meditating after work or school because it helps them let go of the tensions of the day.

There are still others who opt to meditate right before bed in order to allow their unconscious minds to work on their intentions while they sleep. Some people will find this time difficult because they are tired and have to fight their desire to fall asleep.

Choose the time of day that works for you best. This might involve some trial and error, but once you find your ideal time, it will nurture your meditative practice for months or even years to come.

Get comfortable and sit correctly

First, choose comfortable clothes that will not restrict or confine you. Make sure that the area you have designated as your meditation sanctuary is warm.

The way you sit during meditation is extremely important because the emotions and mental state that you experience during meditation are ultimately attributed to the way you hold your body. Even something as intricate as the angle at which you hold your chin can affect how much thinking you do. This is why one of the basic things you need to learn is how to sit properly.

There are two vitally important principles you need to remember in setting up a suitable posture for meditation:

Your posture has to allow you to be comfortable and relaxed

Your posture has to allow you to be alert and aware.

If you are uncomfortable, you won't be able to meditate. If you can't relax, you won't be able to enjoy your meditation.

You might consider sitting cross-legged on a meditation pillow. However, if you are not very flexible, you will probably suffer from doing this. Your best bet is to sit in a chair that you find comfortable and that allows you to sit upright. Here are some elements of good posture that you should consider when sitting.

Your spine should be relaxed and upright.

Avoid slouching because a slumped-over posture closes off your heart. You want your heart and mind to be open during your meditation.

Your shoulders should feel loose yet rolled back and down a little bit

Your hands should sit on your lap, on the arms of a chair, or rest on a cushion.

Your head should be straight with your chin tucked in slightly and the back of your neck should feel long and loose.

Your face should be free of tension and your jaw loses.

Have your feet flat on the floor.

There are special meditation chairs available that will help you sit comfortably and achieve an optimum posture. You can search "meditation chairs" online to see what's available.

Avoid meditating right after a big meal

Research studies show that mental activity is intensified when the body is metabolizing food. To avoid unnecessary noise in your head, choose not to do your meditation right after a big meal.

Don't rush off after meditation

After completing your meditation, sit quietly for a little while longer. Use this time to assimilate your experience as well as reflect and contemplate on it. Be conscious of the intuition or revelation that you might be feeling.

Doing this enables you to fully embrace your meditative experience. It also acts as a gateway for allowing the experience to become part of your 'real world' rather than keeping it as something separate from your day-to-day life. As you learn to listen to your inner voice, your 'real self' will begin to guide you on a daily basis.

Make meditation a daily habit

The benefits you will gain from meditation are cumulative. This means that as you continue to meditate regularly, you will acquire more and more benefits.

If you are truly serious about improving yourself through meditation, make it a part of your daily routine by meditating at least once or twice per day. The rewards you gain will improve with commitment and regularity.

Chapter 5: The 5 steps to proper meditation

Be comfortable

One of the most important first steps in learning to meditate is that you need to be comfortable. If you are not comfortable, you're going to notice every little nuisance. You're going to focus on all of the annoyances that bother you.

Take, for example, a long drive. Whether you're behind the wheel or in the passenger's seat. If you're not comfortable, do you tend to pay attention to much of what's going on around you or what's passing by along the highway? No, you focus on what's not making you comfortable. It could be that the seat is not ideally situated for you or that you have an itch in the middle of your back that you can't scratch or that it's just too hot or cold in the car.

No matter what it is, when you can't get comfortable, it is going to make everything else more challenging for you to enjoy and it is going to make it that much more difficult to *relax*.

And relaxation is the key to meditation.

Look for a place where you can be comfortable. It could be a favorite chair, a room that you enjoy spending time in or even floating around in the pool (though you should avoid any outdoor spaces for the moment because there are always going to be some distractions when you're outside, such as a bird chirping, loud car cruising down the road that you hear, a plane flying overhead, and so forth.

Determine where you'll be most comfortable. This should be a place where you know that when you're sitting down, there aren't going to be things jabbing your back or sides and that your body will be more comfortable than anywhere else.

This comfortable location should also be quiet. If you have other people living in your homes, such as a spouse or children, you want to be able to close the door to this room and make sure that they know when it's close for such and such a time so that they are not to bother you, even to ask a question.

If they don't respect this request, then you may need to find another place to meditate where you won't be bothered.

If you have children and they are going to be trampling around the house, those bangs and crashes are going to be distracting. It will make your process more uncomfortable and much more challenging.

Why is being comfortable and quiet so important to meditation?

As I mentioned, this is especially true when you're first starting out learning how to meditate. Meditation is about relaxing and calming the mind, clearing out all thoughts. If you hear a noise or notice something that is making you uncomfortable, your mind will latch onto that rather than letting go and letting things clear away.

Once you become more comfortable with the process of meditation, you will find that you don't need things to be as ideal, but for now, if you don't find comfort and quiet, you'll struggle and that often leads to people giving up trying to meditate to achieve mindfulness.

Posture

How you sit or stand is a vital factor for many reasons. When you were growing up, you likely heard from your parents or your doctor or even a teacher that you need to stand up straight, that you should sit up straight, and that you should have good posture.

This can help you with many things in life, such as your physical condition and health as well as confidence (a person who has the straight posture and squared shoulders will tend to exude more confidence than someone who slouches).

When you're getting ready to meditate, you need to have good posture. Having good posture allows your body to function at its optimal level. You can take in air and exhale much easier when you're sitting up straight. Your heart will have to work less to move blood throughout your body. Your internal organs will get a break from the constant slouching that you may do at the desk or in the car.

You don't really need to sit on the floor with your legs crossed, but you should focus on keeping your back straight, shoulders square, and chest open. If you feel that you're beginning to drift over during the process, make a slight adjustment and open that chest area back up and get back into a good posture.

While you may already have good posture, for the most part, you will notice that when you begin meditating and relaxing, you may begin to drift down and lose that good posture.

Throughout the meditative process, good posture will be important to help you connect the mind and body so that you can really achieve the goals of this process.

Attention

You don't need to keep your eyes closed when you meditate, but it can help. The only problem with keeping your eyes closed in the beginning is that since you won't have a visual focal point in your sights, your mind could begin trying to fill in the blank space with a host of images or memories.

The main goal at the beginning of this process is to *clear the mind*, so when you give the brain more playing space, more permission to be creative and go wandering through the memories of your past, you're going to find that it's a bit more challenging to clear thoughts away when you keep your eyes closed.

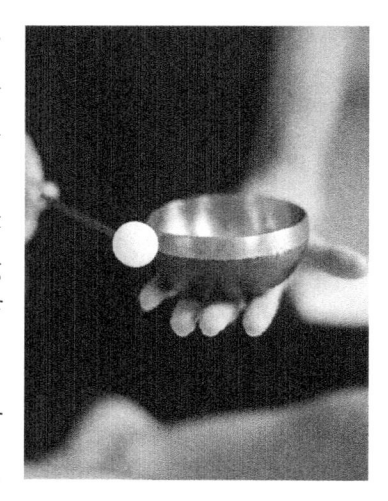

So find something on which to focus your gaze. It could be anything, really. It could be a stain on the carpeting (though that will be more likely to draw your body down into bad posture when you're looking down). It could be a painting on the wall (though you should avoid studying entire images). It could be the corner of a desk or the edge of the TV.

Find something that is just a small piece to focus on. As with the painting or picture on the wall, focus on the edge of the frame and not on the image. If you find that you can't concentrate because the image is in your field of vision and it keeps bringing you back to those memories, then you should either remove it from the wall or shelf and only focus on a dot or the hook in the wall, or find another point on which to focus.

You're going to find that once you begin this process when you are focusing your attention, it's going to wander from time to time. That's natural. When that happens, you simply want to bring your gaze and attention back to the original starting point without a great deal of fuss.

Breath

Breathing is one of the most important aspects of preparing for meditation. While we don't tend to focus much on our breathing during our lives, when you're meditating, you will.

The best breathing technique to use when you're preparing to meditate is deep, slow breaths that come in through the nose and then slowly are released through the mouth.

Some people claim that making the shape of an 'O' with your lips is the best way to exhale, but you can just part your lips slowly (as though you're anticipating a sweet, soft kiss) and allow the air to escape from your body.

Some people also advocate for 'forcing' the air from your body, but that is one more thing that could distract you from what you need to do. As long as you take in long, deep breaths through your nose and then release them from your mouth, your body will start to relax.

53

If this process sounds familiar, it's because it is the common approach for people who are dealing with anxiety or anger issues. If you feel that you're losing control, people will tell you to breathe in through your nose and out through your mouth to *allow the body to relax*.

That's the goal of meditation, so it is right in line with that general way of thinking.

Thoughts

Now, when you are beginning the process of meditating, you need to learn how to push away all thoughts from your mind. This is much easier to say than do, but with practice, you'll be able to do it.

Anything that you're currently thinking about right now should be pushed aside. If you begin thinking about work or something that you forgot to do, you need to push that thought aside.

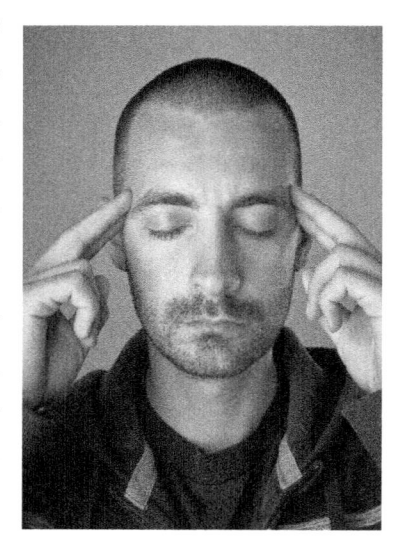

The goal is to achieve peace with no thoughts, no images, no memories. Just emptiness in your mind.

There are many different ways that people set out to achieve this blankness of the mind. Some will find that when they have a thought sneaking in if they only turn that thought into the perception of a physical object (in their mind) and then imagine pushing it out of the room, that helps.

Other people focus on bringing darkness over all thoughts in their minds. You will need to find what works best for you. You'll notice that when you first begin trying to meditate that you *can* clear your mind of all thought and memory, at least for a few moments.

Keeping it that way is the challenge. Practice and experiment with different ways to achieve this goal. When you find something that works for you, you'll know it.

Chapter 6: Types of meditation

Auditory meditation

Auditory meditation is a type of meditation in which the practitioner listens to sound, specifically music or a mantra, in order to achieve peace and concentration.

In this type of meditation, youtube videos can greatly help concentration and improve the meditation experience. This type of meditation is well suitable for people who are eager to learn and interested in learning different forms of mediation.

Auditory meditation is actually not a new fad and has been used by many people in the past, particularly Indian yogis and monks who would listen to parts of their favorite Sanskrit mantras while meditating.

In recent years, more and more people have enjoyed the benefits that auditory meditation can offer. Many people have used this to calm themselves in a very busy world. It is important to seek out a high-quality MP3 player with good sound recording quality so that you can fully merge yourself with the sound of your choice. Look for MP3 players that offer high-quality tones like those offered by Apple Inc. (You can refer to our Youtube channel https://bit.ly/3dyv5u7 so you can try this kind of meditation).

Body scan meditation

Body scan meditation is also a component of mindfulness meditation. Its purpose is to make you aware of the different regions of your body and sensitive to how each part feels. This heightens your ability to connect with your body and to be present with what is going on in the moment. It also helps you cultivate your power to concentrate.

True mind-body awareness doesn't judge the body or its aches and tensions. Rather it simply allows you to say 'hello' to your body with an awareness that enables you to let go of any tension, stress, or illness that you may be harboring.

The object of a body scan meditation is to help you see your body as a perfect whole united by the breath that is flowing in and out of you. It also enables you to tap into the rich sensory experience of being one with your body. As tension is replaced by relaxation and peace, centeredness and wholeness of body, mind, and spirit emerge.

How to do a body scan meditation

In order to practice body scan meditation, begin by lying on the floor, on a mat, or on your bed, or sitting tall with your feet on the floor. Begin with your left toes. Be sensitive to how they feel. Do they feel tense? Focus each exhale on this area of your body and direct your breathing deep into your toes.

You can also try flexing your toes for a few seconds and then relaxing them in order to gain a greater awareness of this area of your body. Next, move your attention to your heel, focusing your breath on your left heel.

Repeat this same process with the arch of your foot, your calf, knee, and thigh, and then do the same thing also with your right leg. Take your time with each region of your body and focus on each part as intently and sensitively as you can. If your mind wanders, gently lead your awareness back to the area of your body that you are on.

After scanning your legs, direct your awareness and breath to your pelvis, then your lower back, abdomen, chest, shoulders, arms, hands, neck, and head. During this process, it is also important to be sensitive to sensations such as the feeling of a blanket or body tingling.

When you have finished scanning the individual parts of your body, unite them by reflecting on the unification of your fingers with your hands and your arms and so on. Be present to your body as a unified whole and allow yourself to relax even more into the connectedness of your entire being.

When you feel it's time to complete your body scan meditation, slowly begin to roll your shoulders, then gently wiggle your fingers and toes, and then slowly begin moving your arms and then your legs. Remain in the present moment as you move from your body scan meditation into the rest of your day or evening.

Meditation for a good night's sleep

Meditation for good sleep is used by people who have trouble sleeping. It can be used either to get to sleep easier or faster or to have a deeper, more restful sleep. Some people use it to meditate and avoid disturbing others during the night if they struggle to fall asleep.

If it does not disturb the people around you, you can listen to some types of music to encourage this meditation. Usually this is music with nature sounds (referred to as white sounds) that promote relaxation. You can refer to our dedicated YouTube session.

https://bit.ly/3dyv5u7

Guided Meditation for Deep Night Sleep

This meditation is best done as the last activity of the day to help you relax into a deep sleep. Before you begin, do whatever you need to and settle down in your bed. Lie down with your legs stretched out to the front and hands resting beside your body. It is best not to wear earphones with this one as you may fall asleep in the middle.

Settle down into your pose and let's begin.

Make a mental scan of the whole of your body and notice how you feel emotionally and physically.

(10 seconds)

Check for any pain or tension in your body. Check for any tiredness.

(10 seconds)

Move your attention from one part of the body to the next from head to toes.

(60 seconds)

During this meditation for deep night sleep, we will concentrate on quieting the mind and releasing the tension in your body. This will help to calm your mind and you will drift into a restful sleep.

Now, take a deep breath and hold it in for a few seconds.

(6 seconds)

Slowly exhale the air, and allow all the tension in your body to leave.

(6 seconds)

Become aware of your thoughts.

(5 seconds)

What are you thinking about?

Are you thinking of your plans for the next day or your day's activities?

Are you feeling worried about someone or something, perhaps?

Just notice your thoughts as they arise and go away, then new ones arise and go away.

(60 seconds)

For a moment, allow your mind the freedom to think.

Let it roam freely and accept all the thoughts that come to it.

(30 seconds)

Let your mind be free to worry about all the challenges in your life.

(10 seconds)

Think of the people you love.

(10 seconds)

Think of your career, job, calling or business.

(10 seconds)

Think of your relationships.

(10 seconds)

Do you have a pet, perhaps? Think about it.

(10 seconds)

Think of the long-overdue plans and goals that you have not accomplished yet.

(10 seconds)

Do not limit your mind.

Let it roam freely.

(60 seconds)

All those thoughts are legit, but for now, we will let them be and not dwell on them.

It is time to allow your mental chatter to quieten or slow down so that you can have a relaxing sleep.

Resting sufficiently will energize your body and mind to enable you to carry on tomorrow's roles and duties properly.

(5 seconds)

Now, become aware of how your body feels at this present moment.

(10 seconds)

Do you feel tired and tense in any part of your body?

Notice the parts that feel tired.

(30 seconds)

Direct your attention to those parts one by one.

Take a deep breath, and as you exhale, visualize all the tension leaving each part.

(30 seconds)

Continue to breathe deeply, and with every exhale, visualize all the tension leaving the tensed part of the body.

(30 seconds)

Become aware of how a sense of relaxation and ease in your body.

Allow the feeling of relaxation to grow throughout your body.

(10 seconds)

With each breath, you take, visualize as the feeling of relaxation spreads across your body.

(20 seconds)

Now, bring your attention to your right heel, where it makes contact with the ground.

Don't move it; use your imagination.

Send awareness to the right foot's big toe.

(5 seconds)

Now send your awareness to the second toe, third, fourth, and pinkie.

(5 seconds)

Become aware of the whole right foot.

Let go of any tension you may be held to on the left foot.

(5 seconds)

Now bring your awareness to the calf on your right leg.

(5 seconds)

Notice the ankles and bring your awareness upwards to the shin.

(5 seconds)

Let the awareness flow to your right knee and feel it softening and relaxing.

(5 seconds)

Now, bring your awareness to your right thigh.

Feel the front of the thigh, the back, and the thigh bone. Hold the entire right thigh in awareness.

(10 seconds)

Take your awareness to your right buttock.

Let it become heavy and then relax.

(5 seconds)

Now move your awareness to your left buttock. Let it become heavy and then relax.

(5 seconds)

Become aware of the left thigh. Notice the top, bottom, and entire bone of your left thigh. Allow it to let go of any tension and relax.

(10 seconds)

Drop your attention downwards to your left knee. Imagine the knee cap softening.

(10 seconds)

Bring your awareness to the left shin all the way down to the ankles.

(5 seconds)

Notice the left calf and let it relax.

(5 seconds)

Scan the entire left leg from the thigh to the ankle.

(10 seconds)

Bring your awareness to the left heel. Allow it to be heavy. Feel the sole of your left foot and let go of any tension

(10 seconds)

Become aware of the big toe on your left foot.

(5 seconds)

Move your awareness to the second toe, third, fourth, and pinkie.

(5 seconds)

Let the whole foot relax.

(5 seconds)

Notice both legs from the buttocks, thighs, knees, calves, shins, ankles, and feet to the toes lying heavy and relaxed on the surface beneath you. Allow both legs to relax completely.

(20 seconds)

Now, become aware of your belly. Do you know how your stomach unravels when you are hungry?

Now, imagine it unraveling and relaxing.

Visualize your entire belly area, the muscles and organs becoming relaxed.

(15 seconds)

Now move your attention to your chest. From the ribs up to the collarbones.

Visualize your entire chest area, the muscles and organs becoming relaxed.

(15 seconds)

Bring your attention to your lower back. Now, move it up from the lower back to the bottom of your neck, allowing the entire back to relax.

(5 seconds)

Notice both shoulders and allow them to completely relax.

(5 seconds)

Bring your awareness to your right-hand bicep, then the tricep and allow your upper arm to relax.

(5 seconds)

Become aware of your elbow and let it relax.

(5 seconds)

Let the right forearm relax.

(5 seconds)

Now, bring your awareness to the right wrist and let it relax.

(5 seconds)

Slowly move your awareness to the palm of your right hand and the back of your right hand.

(5 seconds)

Bring your attention to your right thumb, then the second finger, to the middle finger, ring finger and pinkie.

(5 seconds)

Become aware of the entire right hand and let it relax.

(5 seconds)

Now, take your awareness to the left bicep and tricep and let it relax.

(5 seconds)

Become aware of your elbow and let it relax.

(5 seconds)

Let the left forearm relax.

(5 seconds)

Now, bring your awareness to the left wrist and let it relax.

(5 seconds)

Slowly move your awareness to the palm of your left hand and the back of your left hand.

(5 seconds)

Bring your attention to your left thumb, then the second finger, to the middle finger, ring finger and pinkie

(5 seconds)

Become aware of the entire left hand and let it relax.

(5 seconds)

Feel your whole body on the left side.

Allow it to get heavy and relaxed.

(10 seconds)

Feel your whole body on the right side.

Allow it to get heavy and relaxed.

(10 seconds)

Bring your attention to your neck. Imagine that your neck is lengthening and releasing any tension.

(5 seconds)

notice your entire scalp and it relaxes.

(5 seconds)

Bring your attention to your face. The forehead, cheeks, ears, jaw, chin, lips and nose. Allow the entire face to relax.

(5 seconds)

Take your attention to your right eye and then the left eye. Notice if you have tightly shut the eyelids and allow them to relax.

(5 seconds)

Notice how your body feels now. Is it relaxed? Are there parts that are still tensed?

(5 seconds)

Send relaxing energy to the tensed parts.

(20 seconds)

Calmly say, "I am relaxed" three times.

(20 seconds)

Now, concentrate on counting.

Start at number one and count up to ten. Allow your body to relax even more with each number that passes.

Let us count together, slowly paying attention to each number and your body.

1

Feel your body become more relaxed.

(5 seconds)

2

Notice the peace and calm that surrounds it.

(5 seconds)

3

Feel all the tension leaving, and in its place comes relaxation.

(5 seconds)

Visualize number 4 and notice how your legs and arms are relaxed and heavy.

(5 seconds)

5- Feel a deep wave of relaxation washing over you.

(5 seconds)

6- Your body is deeply relaxed and peaceful.

(5 seconds)

7- Your mind is free from all baggage.

(5 seconds)

8- Relaxed and heavy

(5 seconds)

9- Let your mind float and relax.

(5 seconds)

10- You have reached a level of deep relaxation.

(5 seconds)

Now begin to count backward from 10 to one.

(2 seconds)

Begin from 10 and slowly count nine and continue on your own.

(60 seconds)

You are now peaceful

-comfortable

(2 seconds)

-warm

(2 seconds)

-relaxed

(2 seconds)

-heavy

(2 seconds)

Accept this feeling

(2 seconds)

Nurturing

(2 seconds)

Confident

(2 seconds)

Quiet

(2 seconds)

Smooth

(2 seconds)

You are at peace with yourself

(2 seconds)

You are now fully relaxed, and you can now drift off to deep sleep.

Drift off to sleep- deep and restful sleep.

Goodnight.

Visualization has long been considered to be an effective way of creating positive change because of the mind's ability to vividly imagine what one wants to achieve and also because of the tremendous power of suggestion that it generates. With repetition, visualization is the vehicle that moves you from the imagined state to a shift in your perception of reality. It is this shift that will stimulate new behavior patterns to produce the desired result.

The cocoon imagery is one that is often used. Imagine yourself completely encased in a cocoon that is radiating a bright white light. The light surrounds your entire body until it begins to saturate your being – breathe it in and imagine it permeating every cell of your body, the light glowing through your pores. You are totally bathed in the radiant white light, and it fills you with a feeling of serenity and bliss.

You can remain in this calming, restorative state for the duration of the session, or you can add the dimension of expelling a troubling emotion or problem. It may even be used for healing meditation. While you are surrounded by the cleansing, pure light, you can imagine the problem, addiction, or disease being expelled from your body as black smoke being exhaled through your nostrils or your mouth and losing its potency as it drifts upward and diffuses into the air. You can also envision the negativity as black liquid being forced out by the light and oozing out of your body before being absorbed into the earth without a trace.

A similar concept can be applied using the shrinking box imagery. Imagine a plain, large carton box, open the box, and one by one, begin to place your problems or negative emotions within the box. Once all the objects of negativity are placed in the box, close the box and visualize it becoming smaller and smaller until it eventually disappears.

Visualization as a technique will only be effective with repetition. It will achieve the goal of creating the reality that you desire and rid you of any burdensome problems that you may be experiencing.

Chapter 7: The 7 Most Effective Meditation Techniques

Mindfulness meditation (Vipassana)

Mindfulness meditation (Vipassana : āvaraṇa ॐ) is a central practice in Buddhism, and is considered one of the three core factors leading to Enlightenment. Traditionally, it is practiced as full or half-hour-long sessions. Theoretical benefits are enhanced cognitive awareness, cognitive space/time perception, regulation of attention by distraction and control over thought flow, calm, and clarity during stressful times.

Mindfulness is a practice that has been around for about 2,500 years. While it may have started officially as an aspect of Eastern religious philosophies, it is actually an act of being aware and paying attention to yourself and your surroundings. It's so natural a behavior that we take it for granted because we do it every day without thinking about it. What we fail to do is acknowledge what we are seeing and feeling most of the time. When you add mindfulness to meditation, you add the benefit of acknowledging that you have thoughts and feelings within your mind and body and that it is okay. We don't always like our thoughts or sensations; however, they are there and it does no good to ignore them. Instead, with mindfulness meditation, you open your heart and mind to accept these thoughts and sensations for what they are, without judgment, and seek a way to work through them.

Mindfulness meditation forces you to remain in the here and now and develop better attention to the details of who you are. Meditation is not about sitting still for extended periods of time with nothing at all on your mind because that is not how our minds work. It is estimated that the average adult mind has around 60,000 thoughts a day. That's a lot of thinking going on up there with no off switch. And we do not strive to actually turn the mind off because we truly need the brain to function continuously to keep our organs functioning properly. With meditation, we strive to focus those thoughts in a more useful manner. Mindful meditation allows us to look at some of those thoughts from a distance, acknowledge them without reacting to them, and note how they affect other parts of our body as this process occurs. Then when we step away from the meditative state, we are calmer and better equipped to handle our stressors based on factual reality instead of emotional turmoil.

There are several mindfulness meditation exercises you can try to gain a better understanding of how this works. You can do these exercises alone as a short meditation or incorporate them as part of a longer meditative session. You can do them formally or informally at any time and any place that they benefit you. Try a few out and see how you feel afterward.

Eating Mindfully: Take a piece of your favorite food. First, observe it with your eyes. Notice the color, the shape, and the texture. Touch it with your finger(s). Is it hot, cold, hard, soft, or smooth? Think about the muscles in your arm and hand that are working right now. Think about what the food feels like and then pick it up and smell it. Think about the smell (or lack of smell). Listen to it. Does it make a sound of any kind when you roll it between your fingers? Now touch it to your lips. Does it feel different on your lips than it does on your fingers? Now place it into your mouth. Roll it around for a minute. Think about how it feels, tastes, and interacts with your teeth and tongue. Feel your jaw muscles moving around. Go ahead and chew it. Feel how it breaks apart in your mouth before you swallow it. Close your eyes and picture it going down your throat and into your stomach.

Have you ever experienced your food in this manner before? By being mindful of the process of eating a single bite of food, you open your mind to new experiences about the actual food item. It may now taste differently than you thought it would. Try this with other types of food and see if you get similar results.

Walking Mindfully: Every day, most people walk some place at some point. Whether it's down the aisle at a grocery store, down the hallway in an office building, down your driveway, or through a park, there is a variety of opportunities to experience mindful walking. Wherever you choose to experiment with this technique, the goal is to allow yourself time to observe everything in the environment around you and how you react to it. Look at the sky. Note the color. Are there clouds? Is it bright or gloomy? How does that make you feel? Look at the surface you are walking on. Is it dirt, grass, rock, paved, or some other substance? How does it feel under your feet? Does it make a sound with each footfall? Are you warm or cold or comfortable? Are you alone or are there other people? What noises do you hear? Are you soothed or agitated by the noises you hear? Try and observe every little detail about everything within your sight. Textures, smells, sounds, and maybe even tastes or odors in the air as they all play a part in how you will feel once you are done walking. When you are done walking, think about how different this walk was compared to the last time you walked a similar path. Being mindful causes you to heighten your awareness of the physical world around you and become more in tune with nature or the lack of nature.

Mindful Conversation: We all talk to other people every day, whether it's with other adults, strangers, friends, children, family members, professionals, co-workers, or any other host of possible contacts. Most of the time, we speak without a lot of forethought, which sometimes causes us stress in the long run. We have all said something at some point that we wish we could take back, but alas, the time machine has not been built yet and we are not allowed to take the proverbial foot out of our mouths. With mindful conversations, we pay extra attention to body language and words that have been spoken and allow ourselves a minute to think about our response based on what we would feel like if our response was directed at ourselves. It is a hard practice to master but well worth the effort. This mindful technique is best practiced with a friend that is willing to give you a minute to formulate your response after you have actually thought about what you are going to say (versus just blurting out whatever comes into your head like people normally do). You put yourself in the other person's position mentally to see how you would feel about your response to any statement prior to making that response. In other words, you become mindful of how other people might feel. This exercise helps you build compassion for your fellow human beings. No one wants to be the bad guy in any relationship and even close friends sometimes mess up and say the wrong thing. We are, after all, human and tend to let our emotions react for us instead of us having control of our emotions. We tend to make judgments of people without enough facts to support our belief and then, instead of really listening to what that person is saying, we become distracted by trying to prove that the person is as bad as we want to believe they are. If you are using mindful conversation, you will stay focused on exactly what is being said without adding your own judgments and creating opinions in your own mind of what you think the other person is trying to tell you. So for this exercise, you first listen intently to the other person, and after they have finished speaking (and only after), you then think about how you are going to respond in a manner that is non-judgmental, asking yourself how you would feel and what kind of a response would you want to hear. Once you have done this, you repeat the process. It is not easy. We may have two ears, but we tend to talk twice as much as we listen. And our mind tends to get out of control by thinking of responses well before another person has finished speaking, thereby causing us to miss the point most of the time. The mindful conversation is as much about learning to listen as it is about learning to respond.

Mindfulness can and should be practiced every day. It makes life much more enjoyable when you learn to appreciate the details of life as they occur around you on an ongoing basis. Mindfulness in meditation causes you to focus your thought processes on a single process at a time for the maximum benefit while also allowing us to realize that the mind will continue to randomly roam to places where we wish it would not. Mindful meditation allows us to focus on this minute, right here, right now, without discounting the stress of yesterday or tomorrow. We still acknowledge the thoughts that pass through our minds and acknowledge that emotions go with those thoughts, but we also remind ourselves that there is a time to deal with them just beyond the minutes of meditation.

Walking meditation

This is another form of mindfulness meditation that's exceptionally great for stress relief. This technique is as simple as taking a walk outside and has the added benefit of giving you some exercise and fresh air. Walking meditation is so effective because it helps you put physical distance between you and your worries as well as mental and emotional distance. This technique also forces you to put aside time for yourself.

Combining the act of walking with meditation may be considered a metaphor for life we aim to achieve. It is a life lived with greater awareness and mindfulness even as we go about our regular activities and daily interactions. We tend to walk or move from place to place with a destination in mind. Most of us live goal-driven lives that have left us burnt out and stress-ridden. Walking meditation brings our complete attention to the act of walking, we will arrive at our destination, but the destination itself becomes secondary to the journey.

The primary goal in your walking meditation session is to stay mindful at each moment. There is no 'right' way or location or even distance to walk, but it does require some planning to gain as much as possible from experience. You may consider walking indoors, which offers the best opportunity for you to control your environment in terms of ambient noises, which can become a distraction when outdoors. Of course, walking outdoors in a park or even in your garden if you have a large enough area, can be quite pleasant. Pre-determine the area or distance that you will cover so, you will not have to make a decision while walking. For a beginner, it is usually helpful to punctuate your walking area with several required turns; for example, you may walk back and forth on a shorter route or walk along a path that allows you to move as if along the lines of a square. Each time you stop to make that turn, pause and bring your awareness back to the object of your meditation in case your mind has drifted.

You can decide on the best place for your walk after you have tried it in different ways – each pace has its particular advantage. A slower pace can help to limit distractions; you can keep your lids half-closed without creating anxiety that you may bump into anything. You can coordinate your movements with your breathing which also helps with maintaining focus. At this pace, however, it is possible to get a feeling of being unbalanced as it is not a pace that comes naturally to the body.

A more natural pace can also be used – that would be your regular walking pace. At this pace, you may be less inclined to keep your eyes half-closed, so it gives you a wider angle for your eyes and thus your mind to wander. However, you can counteract that by labeling your steps as you make them keep your mind focused; try saying "step…step…step" in time with your movements.

Once you have planned your route and are ready to go, take a deep breath and bring awareness to your body – release any tension in your jaw and neck. Your arms should be hanging naturally at your sides, and your legs should feel relaxed. Without focusing on your feet, look downward at an angle of a few feet in front of you. Your gaze should not be fixed but should allow as small a visual cone as possible to avoid distractions. Begin walking and bring your complete attention to your lower legs and feet. Feel your feet as they make contact with the ground, the sensation of your heel touching the ground before rolling the ball of the foot downward. Bring awareness to the contraction of your leg as you lift it and how it feels as it moves through the air and back to placement. If you are walking barefoot, then you will have other sensations associated with each step, the feel of the carpet under your feet or the coolness of the floor tile. The important thing is to bring mindfulness to the act of walking; because it is such a natural process, the mind is prone to wander; just bring it back gently when you become aware of it.

Some meditators use walking meditation as a natural precursor for their regular meditation because the rhythmic movement helps to focus the mind and sets the stage for a productive session. This is a great way to start your session but engaging in just walking meditation can also yield amazing results. Another advantage of this method is that you can easily incorporate it at other times during your day when you have the opportunity to move from place to place, and this act of mindful walking will continually develop your skills of mindfulness and awareness.

How to do a walking meditation

Not all meditation requires you to remain still during a session. Walking meditation, for example, can be just as profound as a still meditation.

For a walking meditation, the main object of the meditation is your walking movements. The alternating left-right steps create a meditative state.

In order to perform a walking meditation, set aside 20 minutes in which you can solely focus on your meditation. It is best not to combine it with trying to get somewhere, running errands, or exercising.

Before you begin, stand still and take some deep breaths. Direct your full attention to your breathing. At the same time, become aware of your body, how it feels standing, and the sensations going on inside of it, and then allow your breathing to return to normal.

Next, begin walking at a slow but normal pace. Keep your attention focused on the sensations in your body as you walk. Notice how your feet feel connecting with the earth. Notice how your arms feel swaying at your sides. Also, take note of what your energy feels like inside your body.

You can even go further than this and scan all the parts of your body, the soles of your feet, your ankles, knees, chest, shoulders, fingertips, neck, and face as you walk. If you feel tension anywhere, let it go by consciously relaxing that part of your body. When your mind wanders, don't worry. Gently bring it back to the left-right-left motion of walking.

A labyrinth can also be a very effective meditative practice. Before you begin walking a labyrinth, take a moment to transition from your daily life to the labyrinth experience. Stand still and breathe deeply, then slowly return your breath to normal.

You can set an intention for the experience: questions, feelings, affirmations, or you can simply walk and see what the experience brings. The nice thing about a labyrinth is that it takes you out of your linear life experience. It mirrors the twists and turns of life and allows you to relax into them rather than resist them.

You can also set your focus on letting things go while you walk the labyrinth and then focus on what you will bring out from the center and back into your life.

Alternatively, you can use the walking body scan meditation (previously mentioned in this section) while walking the labyrinth.

Practice

To practice walking meditation, you'll need to find a park, beach, forest, or safe neighborhood where you'll feel safe and comfortable walking by yourself. You'll also have to make sure your shoes are suitable for walking and your clothes are comfortable. The suggested length of your walk is thirty minutes, but you can make it shorter or longer depending on what you want and how much time you have available. You may want to set the alarm for yourself on your phone, and if your surroundings are too noisy, you can use earphones to listen to a guided meditation or soothing music.

1. Make sure you won't be interrupted on your walk, and your phone is switched to silent so you won't be bothered by calls and messages. Start your meditation practice by walking at a pace you're comfortable with. Most people prefer walking fairly slowly, so they can concentrate better, but you're welcome to speed it up if that works better for you.
2. As you walk, start to focus on the movement of your body. Feel the earth beneath you with every step you take, the wind in your eyes, and the swing of your arms as you walk.
3. You can start focusing on your breathing as well and even try to synchronize your breathing and your footsteps. Try taking two steps every time you inhale and another two every time you exhale. If you get distracted by thoughts of all your problems or things that tend to stress you out, or if your mind begins to wander, simply acknowledge the thoughts or take note of where your mind is going and refocus yourself.
4. If you're not heading towards a specific destination, or you haven't planned a route that brings you back to where you started, you'll have to turn around and walk back at some point. When your time is up or you've reached the end of your walk, end your meditation by letting your mind slip out of the meditative trance. Walking a little quicker for a few steps is a good way to help you get that done.

Zen meditation

The main idea of zen derives from the Chinese philosophy of Taoism — the belief that everything in nature is connected and has the meaning".

Zen Buddhism was imported into Japan after China's invasion by Kublai Kahn (1239-1294). Since then, Zen has become very popular in Japan. Zen meditation was once only practiced by monks and priests. Today, people all around the world practice zen meditation even though they are not associated with religion. Meditation is known to be a great way to unwind, stimulate the imagination and achieve mental concentration.

Zen meditation is a lot like other types of meditation but there are some differences that may catch you off guard:

In traditional forms of meditation, there are three stages:

Briefly labeling these as "watching," "chanting," and "centering" will do for now.

In Zazen, the stages are:

Preparation or getting ready for the meditation. This is one of the few examples in martial arts training where a warmup is considered an important part of the process. The body needs to get ready for four hours of sitting; it cannot relax properly if it is not warmed up properly.

Zen teachers will sometimes suggest 15 or 20 minutes of walking meditation before actually settling into a period of seated zazen. This may be done because normally, beginners are not truly capable of sitting still until they have sat through enough zazen to develop the mental agility necessary to control their bodies while seated quietly and still without excessive physical tension.

Observing. Perhaps the most obvious difference with zen meditation is the use of a simple word, "Namu" or "Nam myoho renge kyo" to start your meditation. Namu is pronounced "naam" and translates in English to

Buddha is teaching me concentration

(for other words, see: Translating Namu)

It may not seem like much, but this simple word serves an important purpose. By saying namu each time you meditate, you are stating that you are actually doing something spiritual while sitting silently and focusing on a point in front of you. This simple change in wording is significant and helps you to overcome the kind of mental resistance you will often feel when you sit silently for any length of time.

Contemplation, is the second part of zen meditation. This stage is usually only done for about two or three minutes at a time, but can be extended indefinitely if you choose. It has the purpose of focusing your mind on a specific subject and exploring its meaning without getting caught up in the subject's history or message.

During this phase all thoughts (good or bad) are allowed, but not allowed to become your focus. The focus should be on your experience while concentrating on that thought. If you find that your mind wanders to another thought, then gently return it to the original thought. Do this until you become comfortable staying with your original thought.

This can be difficult at first, but like all aspects of meditation, you will get better with practice.

Relaxation, which is the final part of zen meditation. This is where you sit comfortably and finally experience what a true period of "relaxation" feels like. You should now be mentally centered and able to relax in ways you never have before. Of course, you may still be a little tense from the mental exertion of observing, contemplating and contemplating-relaxing

At this point, you should begin to realize the benefits of zen meditation. As your mind becomes accustomed to concentrating for longer periods of time and as your body becomes more relaxed and calm, you will find that you are able to meditate for four hours or more without any problems. Also, within this stage, there is another important step:

Contemplation-establishing. This is where you start to notice subtle changes in your consciousness during meditation. You will notice your thoughts becoming calmer, quieter and more focused. Your mind will become more stable in its operations and you will finally feel that zen meditation is something you can use every day to calm your mind.

Upon completing this stage, it is only a matter of repeating the stages of preparation, observation, contemplation and contemplation-establishing until you reach the end of the 4-hour session. This process is repeated every morning when you meditate (if possible) or whenever your mind becomes restless.

This completes an entire session of zen meditation. Those that learn from traditional forms of meditation often have trouble mastering even one full session in a single sitting.

Practice test of zen meditation

If you wish to meditate in a zen way, you can practice this on your own. You should be sitting quietly and peacefully when the bell rings.

When the bell rings, recite the following phrase first: Namu-Buddha is teaching me concentration.

After this, we will go into meditation by reciting the phrases below:

I am listening to the sound of Namu, Buddha, Jinen-myoho-renge-kyo. (it is important to chant it.) The sound of my mind is Namu-Buddha is teaching me concentration.

After this, we will sit in meditation and concentrate on the sound of Namu for about 15 minutes. This is important at first, but later you should be able to concentrate on the sound for a longer period of time. After 15 minutes, we will concentrate on the next phrase:

The sound of my mind is Namu-Buddha is teaching me concentration.

After this, we will sit in meditation and concentrate on the sound of Namu for about 30 minutes. This is important at first, but later, you should be able to concentrate on the sound for a longer period of time. After 30 minutes, we will say:

The sound of my mind is Namu-Buddha is teaching me concentration.

After this, we will sit in meditation and concentrate on the sound of Namu for about 2 hours and then stop.

After that, you should be able to start the whole process again without saying any of the phrases. All you have to do is concentrate on the sound of namu or nam myoho renge kyo and you will be meditating in zen way.

The most important thing is to concentrate on your mind, not on words but when doing it first, it is better if you follow this method straightforwardly.

Transcendental Meditation

Breath is the life force or Prana Shakti. Once you stop breathing, you are no more than a dead body. Control of breath is, therefore, an important aspect of every meditation technique. It is clear that our mind is a monkey. It flits from one thought to another, to the past and into the future. The mind can never be idle. It's like a pot that must contain something. It is filled with air if nothing is poured or kept into it. All meditation techniques are geared toward quietening our minds. The stillness of mind is the ultimate goal. But in today's modern world, we do not have the time or patience to wait. In Transcendental meditation, you are required to chant a mantra during the meditation. Chanting of mantra keeps your mind focused.

Maharishi Mahesh Yogi was an Indian philosopher who introduced Transcendental Meditation (TM) to the world. In this technique, you are given a few words to chant while meditating. Every individual has a unique mantra or chant, which is provided by a trained practitioner or certified TM teacher. Transcendental meditation can only be learned by attending a program conducted by certified teachers. However, the TM technique is so popular that it is taught even in schools.

There are numerous scientific studies conducted to prove the efficacy of Transcendental meditation. Generally, the accepted belief is that practicing Transcendental meditation leads to a calm and composed mind. It is relaxing and rejuvenating. TM is usually practiced twice daily for a period of ten to twenty minutes, once after breakfast and once before lunch.

Transcendental meditation leads to altered consciousness, something akin to Yoga Nidra. Therefore practicing Transcendental meditation can be an effective way to access your subconscious. This, in turn, can change your perspective on life. Many psychological problems like depression can be managed effectively by using Transcendental meditation along with medication.

There are contrarian views regarding the Transcendental meditation technique. Some reports suggest that the effect of TM is as good as keeping your eyes closed. Such a view ignores the fact that TM is not only about keeping your eyes closed. It's much more than that. Ultimately, it's the massive popularity of Transcendental meditation that proves the point – you can't fool all the people all the time. Unless there is a definite health and psychological benefit, people will not follow this meditation benefit blindly or with their eyes closed.

How to practice

If you want to improve your concentration, lower anxiety levels, or even reduce your risk of cancer, transcendental meditation may be the answer.

This type of practice is a form of mindfulness that can help people shift their consciousness from the present time to a meditative state that is said to induce feelings of peace and well-being among those who have had success with it. It could also help you sleep better and feel less stressed. The benefits are vast and far-reaching, so it's no surprise that so many people are embracing this simple technique.

Transcendental Meditation is a simple, natural and effortless technique that allows you to find a source of peace and calm within the mind and body. It is taught and practiced individually, usually in the sitting position with eyes closed. Transcendental meditation does not involve concentration or focus on repeating words, sounds or phrases. It's an innovative technique of meditation that was discovered by Maharishi Mahesh Yogi in India during the 1950s. The practice has been shown to help improve the overall quality of life for those who engage in it on a regular basis.

Transcendental Meditation is done for 10 minutes twice a day while sitting with your eyes closed. It's important to sit with a straight spine and take slow, deep breaths in through the nose and out through the mouth as you focus on your mantra. A mantra is a word or a sound that you repeat silently to yourself inside your head. The most popular mantras are "Om" or "AUM." It can take anywhere from two weeks to six months before you experience any relief from stress, anxiety, or pain.

Transcendental meditation practice has also been shown to help reduce alcohol consumption and cigarette consumption among those who have tried it regularly. It can help people quit smoking as well as provide relief from chronic pain like backaches, headaches and more.

If you're struggling with an addiction of any kind, transcendental meditation could be a solution for you. Many people have found success in overcoming the urge to abuse drugs or alcohol by engaging in this technique. It has also helped people overcome their cravings for food and sweets.

Practice test

Step 1

Find a quiet place where you won't be disturbed by noise, pets or family members. Sit in a comfortable position with your spine straight and your mouth closed. Use a timer to keep track of the time you're meditating. Start with 10 minutes at first, but you can increase the amount of time as you become more comfortable with the practice.

Step 2

Close your eyes and bring your awareness to the breath. Notice how it feels moving in and out of your body. It can be a little bit uncomfortable at first to focus on your breath, but if you practice regularly, you'll start to notice how your mind can wander as you breathe in and out. Some people find it helpful to think of sounds while they focus on their breath. Others say that thinking of anything is fine as long as it isn't a distraction.

Step 3

Once you have spent a few minutes focusing on the breath, begin counting your breaths down from 10 to 1. You may find it helpful to count in three sets of 1-2-3 or 1-2-3-4 until the final number is reached. If you get distracted by a thought, just start counting again from the last number. If a sound comes up, go back to counting your breaths.

Step 4

Once you've reached the final number in your countdown, reset to 10 and start another round of counting down from 10. Don't try to stop thinking or force yourself to think of anything else when you reach zero. This is when many people experience a shift in consciousness, but it is important not to strive for it. The practice will take some time before you feel results like reduced anxiety or stress levels. It may take some time before you begin sleeping better as well.

Dynamic Meditation

Dynamic meditation brings the benefits of meditation into your daily life as it utilizes visualization techniques to create mental exercises that are brief and easy to incorporate into your schedule. With these techniques, you can gain control over your mind through focused breathing or meditation without needing hours of sessions on end.

Dynamic meditation is a technique that incorporates visualization practices, breathing exercises, and various other methods to help control your mental perception from within your daily activities, cutting the time needed for an entire day of meditation down. Why should you practice Dynamic Meditation?

Meditation is an activity that many people find quite simple and easy to do; however, unless you have a long session planned for or a need to satiate your mind for several hours. That leaves little time to give your mind the time it truly needs; with Dynamic Meditation, you can get the same benefit from different types of meditation in just a few minutes each day. As well as taking the time you would have spent meditating, Dynamic Meditation enables you to save even more time at work, in school, driving through traffic, etc. – cutting down on your time wasted each day without sacrificing any of the benefits from meditation.

Dynamic Meditation is a simple technique for attaining and maintaining a positive state of mind without needing to cram meditative sessions into your day. It incorporates visualization techniques to help relax you in the same way meditation does, but allows you to do it within brief moments throughout the day, cutting down on time wasted and adding benefit to your days.

You can use this technique while doing anything at all; on the train, while waiting in line at a store, while walking back from lunch – even while driving! All you need to do is visualize yourself immersed in nature somewhere quiet and peaceful. You can imagine yourself walking down a green forest path or sitting on a bench at the park looking out at the scenery.

The idea behind this technique of Dynamic Meditation is to put your mind into an active, relaxed state where it is in control of its own perception, rather than having it become as anxious and anxious as it would be if you spent hours immersing yourself in meditation – which could lead to many health and mental benefits. In fact, for some people, the benefits are even more pronounced because they are able to utilize Dynamic Meditation without the need for long periods of time; simply using alternative methods from those used in traditional meditation to create relaxation within their daily life.

You will practice Dynamic Meditation by utilizing a technique known as Mindfulness, which helps your mind to become much more aware of its surroundings because it is so focused on being receptive to different stimuli and a wide array of information. To achieve this, you will need to take several deep breaths, focusing on each breath as you exhale. As you inhale, picture yourself in a state of blissful relaxation; basking in the warmth and pleasantness of nature. You can do this by imagining yourself sitting beneath a shade tree, or on a beach watching the waves roll onto shore – allowing all the troubles of your day to melt away, releasing the stress that was built up while doing whatever it is that you are doing.

When you practice this technique regularly it will become more and more easy to do it subconsciously. By using Dynamic Meditation daily, your mind will become more aware of its surroundings, as well as a heightened sense of relaxation and calm that will be with you through your daily activities until you choose to relax again at another time.

How to practice Dynamic Meditation

There are different methods to practice Dynamic Meditation, however all of them involve the same basic principles. In order to practice Dynamic Meditation you will need to think of a spiritual place which makes you feel calm, relaxed and comfortable. This can translate in a number of ways; some believe that meditating in nature is a good way, while others prefer to imagine being in their home at the time they were growing up.

Practice test for Dynamic Meditation

Mindfulness is the main principle of Dynamic Meditation, and it will help you to keep your mind focused on a particular task. It will put you into a state of awareness that is beneficial in the short term but even more beneficial over time as it helps you develop intrinsic awareness. In addition your breathing will become more relaxed, which will work to calm your nerves and help you maintain a more positive state of mind.

To begin practicing Dynamic Meditation, find a quiet and comfortable place where you are free from distraction to allow yourself to fully concentrate on the meditation. If there are any sources of noise in the area around you, try practicing some soft music beforehand so that when it comes time for your meditation session there is nothing but silence.

When you begin to meditate, breathe in deeply; inhaling and exhaling slowly and deeply. Visualize the air entering your body through your nose, filling your lungs with fresh air in a clean environment. As you exhale imagine all the worries, concerns and stress being released from your body.

If you find yourself reverting back into thoughts about work, family or other responsibilities try to bring yourself back to focus on the meditation. If it is easier for you to view pictures of nature around you to help put you at ease, take out a picture of a scene that is calming for you rather than searching online for nature pictures or scrolling through Instagram. If you are having trouble with finding a picture, try searching for "peaceful scenes" on Google Images – you are sure to find some beautiful and relaxing pictures.

When you begin to feel relaxed and comfortable, imagine yourself in the scene that this time releases your mind from the pressures of everyday life. Imagine yourself surrounded by the sounds of nature and feel your body relax as a result.

Next, imagine your worries or concerns leaving your body with that last exhale. You can let everything out or bring to mind any problems you may be facing at this point.

If you find at any point during your meditation that you have lost your focus and can't seem to get back into the flow of the exercise, don't worry. Just try again. Even though it is very easy to fall into a routine of being able to relax instantly from this kind of meditation if you want to make it a daily habit, you will have to continue practicing until you can do it instantly every time.

Some of the best benefits that Dynamic Meditation offers are increased motivation and productivity, as well as more positive outlooks on life in general.

Yoga meditation

Yoga Nidra is a technique to deal with the misperceptions created by our senses. According to the ancient sages, the universe is much bigger than what we can perceive with our senses. Our brain processes images and sounds at the conscious level. However, our subconscious has a bigger role to play in our lives. Our subconscious contains the secret to our future. If you can find a way to your subconscious, you can really and truly achieve happiness. This technique to access your subconscious is called Yoga Nidra.

Yoga Nidra is a powerful meditation technique, a systematic method of inducing complete physical, mental and emotional relaxation. Yoga Nidra is derived from two words - Yoga means single-pointed awareness and Nidra is sleep. This meditation technique has been derived from the Tantras or ancient Indian practice. It was developed by Swami Satyananda Saraswati in Rishikesh, where he had a spiritual experience that triggered his interest in developing the science of Yoga Nidra. Swami later went on to lay the foundation of a new school of Yoga called 'Bihar school of Yoga.

Yoga Nidra, in the words of Swami Satyananda Saraswati, is conscious sleep. Although one looks to be asleep when engaging in Yoga Nidra, one's consciousness is actually operating at a higher degree of awareness. Yoga Nidra is frequently referred to as psychic slumber or deep relaxation with inner consciousness because of this. Contact with the subconscious and unconscious realms happen naturally in this transitional state between sleep and alertness.

The consciousness is not subject to either sleep or waking during yoga Nidra. It is in a state halfway between the two. The word "the hypnagogic state" has been used in modern psychology. However, Swami Satyananda Saraswati prefers to use the term "the hypnagogic state." The mind is incredibly open and responsive in this state. Learning new things, including languages, can happen quickly. The advice given at this stage is effective in getting rid of bad habits and inclinations. Yoga Nidra can actually be used to guide the mind toward achieving anything. This is how renowned yogis and swamis achieve their astounding feats.

One can access intuitions from the unconscious mind by using Yoga Nidra. Inspiration for poetry and art comes from this state. Additionally, it is where the most innovative scientific discoveries come from. To address issues that arose in his work, Wolfgang von Goethe utilized the insights and inspirations that came from this mood. The benzene ring's circular structure was revealed to the discoverer via visions in which a serpent was seen devouring its own tail. In his dreams, Bohr perceived the atomic structure, while Einstein proposed the theory of relativity.

Taking part in Yoga Nidra

A typical Yoga Nidra session lasts between twenty and forty minutes. You must follow the advice of a master or guru. A guided Yoga Nidra recording is available.

Select a quiet area and shut the windows and doors before beginning. Lay down in Shavasana (corpse pose) on a sturdy surface, and pay attention to the directions. Continue mentally carrying out the directions. Simply pay attention to the instructions and mentally carry them out. Do not concentrate or regulate your breathing. The main goal of Yoga Nidra is to avoid falling asleep. If you nod off, you lose the awareness that your practice is meant to cultivate.

Getting ready for the practice

Shavasana, in which the body is not in contact with any of its limbs, decreases touch sensations and is used to practice yoga Nidra. Turning the palms of the hands upwards keeps the fingers, which are very sensitive touch organs, off the ground. Wearing light, loose clothing is recommended. There should be no winds or breezes coming directly at the body, nor should the room be very warm or chilly. Simply closing your eyes will stop visual inputs from happening. The attention then turns to sounds outside. The mind would grow restless and unsettled if all sensory stimuli were forcibly suppressed. As a result, the mind is instructed to focus on external noises and to travel from one sound to another while adopting a witnessing attitude. After some time, the mind gradually grows bored with the outside world and automatically quiets.

Resolve

You must be very careful when selecting your own sankalpa or resolve. The language must be very exact and clear in order to reach the subconscious mind. A few examples of succinct, affirmative, and direct statements are as follows:

I will succeed in everything I do; I will be more alert and effective, I will acquire entire health, I will realize my spiritual potential, and I will be a force for the evolution of others.

Only one Sankalpa should be selected based on your preferences and needs. Be patient and don't rush. After making a decision, you cannot switch to another Sankalpa. Don't count on outcomes right now. Depending on the type of resolve and how deeply it is ingrained in mind, time is needed. The outcome is dependent upon your sincerity and intense desire to fulfill your Sankalpa's purpose.

Consciousness rotation

It does not require any physical movement and is not a technique of concentration to rotate consciousness through the various areas of the body. There are only three requirements to be met during the practice:

Keep your focus, pay attention to the voice, and move your mind quickly.

When you hear the phrase "right-hand thumb," mentally repeat it, focus on the right hand thumb, and then continue. The ability to visualize the various body components is not required. All you need to do is get used to going in the same order, mentally repeating the names of the various bodily parts the way a kid learns to do with the alphabet. You don't need to keep track of what follows next. The subconscious mind is where the entire process happens. The arrangement of the body parts must be automatic, spontaneous, and complete.

The right thumb and little toe of the right foot serve as the starting and stopping points for the rotation of consciousness during Yoga Nidra, followed by the circuit from the left thumb to the little toe of the left foot. From the heels to the back of the head, there are subsequent circuits, and from the head and other facial features to the legs.

Understanding of the breath

Drawing attention to the breath completes the physical relaxing process after these rotations of consciousness are finished. One should not seek to force or alter the breath throughout this exercise; instead, one should simply keep awareness of it. You can keep an eye on your breath in your nostrils, your chest, or the space between your navel and your throat. Typically, counting breaths aloud while doing so leads to increased calm. Not only does breathing awareness encourage calm and focus, but it also awakens higher energies and channels them to each and every cell in the body. It supports pratyahara from the subtle body during the subsequent practices.

Sensations and emotions

The next step is to unwind on the emotional and feeling level. Intensely physical or emotional emotions are recalled or awakened, fully experienced, and then eliminated. Typically, pairings of opposing emotions are used for exercises, such as heat and cold, weight and lightness, pain and pleasure, joy and sadness, and love and hatred. In Yoga Nidra, the pairing of emotions unifies the opposing hemispheres of the brain, balances our fundamental urges, and regulates unconscious processes. Additionally, through reliving memories of intense emotions, this technique fosters emotional willpower and leads to emotional calm through catharsis.

Visualization

Yoga Nidra's final phase promotes mental tranquility. You must imagine the visuals mentioned or explained in the practice section's instructions. The images that are utilized frequently have universal importance and strong associations, bringing the deep unconscious' concealed contents into conscious awareness.

By clearing the mind of upsetting or painful thoughts, visualization exercises help people become more self-aware and relaxed. It encourages mental focus or Dharana. Visualization transitions into dhyana, or pure meditation, at more advanced levels. The difference between the conscious and unconscious selves fades as the perceived item is experienced consciously in the unconscious, and obtrusive images stop appearing.

Terminating the action

An image that inspires intense sensations of tranquility and peace typically serves as the final visualization exercise. Because of this, the unconscious mind is particularly open to suggestions and encouraging thoughts. Yoga Nidra is therefore completed with a resolve. The seed that enables one to significantly alter one's attitude, behavior, and destiny is this direct order from the conscious mind to the unconscious. Clarity and optimism in the resolution statement are crucial. This will strengthen the intellect and promote optimism. One should genuinely believe that their determination will work. The effect of the resolution on the unconscious mind is strengthened by this faith, enabling the resolve to materialize in one's life.

Yoga Nidra is completed by gently pulling the mind out of mental sleep and back into the awake state.

Ho'oponopono meditation

Ho'oponopono is a Hawaiian word meaning "to make right." It is also known as "Hawaiian forgiveness" or "Hawaiian reconciliation." The practice has been used for centuries by Hawaiians with deep spiritual roots and connections to heal physical, mental and emotional pain. It has been used by Hawaiian kahuna (priests) to heal the sick, restore order and forgiveness in interpersonal relationships, and even deliver messages from departed loved ones.

Ho'oponopono, like so many of the world's traditions and indigenous practices, are tools that can be used by each of us to heal ourselves.

What is a Ho'oponopono Mediation?

A Ho'oponopono meditation is a tool that helps us look deep within and discover the blockages preventing us from living a life filled with joy, happiness and peace. It does this by helping us realign ourselves with the universal law of love or "Aloha." Aloha is an ancient Hawaiian word meaning "to love" or "to be in agreement" or "to keep the peace." Taken at face value, Aloha may sound like a simple idea. Aloha is simply a term used to describe love or the universal acceptance, forgiveness and compassion that we all share as human beings, yet somehow it can be difficult to achieve.

This method of healing uses the power of intention and love to dispel those energies which have been artificially created by us that stand in the way of our good health and happiness.

How to practice Ho'oponopono meditation

Ho'oponopono is a powerful and highly spiritual practice which can be used to help us achieve our full potential in the world. This may include some of the things we don't like about ourselves, such as anger, jealousy, hurt, sadness and guilt.

Ho'oponopono asks that we take responsibility for our actions and our inactions. We are each responsible for how we feel, both mentally and physically. When we are unable to forgive others or ourselves for perceived wrongs, it creates suffering in our lives which can manifest as physical ailments or emotional blocks that seem totally out of proportion to what has occurred.

Ho'oponopono, in its most basic form, simply asks that we stop what we are doing and sit quietly. It is also important to feel no need to hurry. A "Ho'oponopono meditation" can be as short as a few minutes or last several hours. The time you spend on your Ho'oponopono meditations may increase with time as you become more familiar with the process and the "cleanings" that occur during this period of quiet reflection.

Every individual is unique, so there is no set formula for using the Ho'oponopono method of reconciliation. There are certain steps that most people use in their efforts to achieve peace.

Steps to Ho'oponopono meditation

1. Sit in any position that is comfortable for you but is not too rigid. Sit up straight and make sure your posture is not rigid. Your back should be relaxed, your shoulders relaxed and your knees should be comfortably bent with no tense leg muscles. Remember that Ho'oponopono meditation works through your energy system, so sit with energy flow flowing freely through you. You may find that it helps to place a pillow on the small of your back or on a small cushion under your buttocks. Experiment, trying different positions until you

find one that feels good to you and best suits the way you hold yourself physically.
2. Close your eyes and start breathing deeply and rhythmically. This is called diaphragmatic breathing.
3. Ask for forgiveness for anything you may have done that has hurt another person or yourself. It may help to think of a specific incident or thought that you would like to be forgiving of and say this out loud in the present tense as if it is happening now. For example, saying, "I am sorry I said nasty things to [insert name here] when I was frustrated."
4. Allow all negative thoughts, emotions, or feelings that you wish to forgive to come into your awareness during this time of quiet reflection. It may help to visualize each of these things as a cloud or a dark fog. You can use the power of intention to ask that this fog be dispelled or diffused.
5. Accept yourself, your present situation and all those involved in this incident for who they are and for what they have done. Aim for forgiveness, not retribution or revenge. Acceptance is the first step to healing and it is often difficult law of attraction to forgive others, especially if you feel like they have wronged you deeply or if you have been hurt by their time and time again. You may find it useful to think about the other person's position and their point of view in order to understand why they felt/feel the way they do. For example, you may be angry because you feel like you were wronged or mistreated in some way and it's impossible to forgive them for this. It is important to realize that the only thing that ever happened was an incident that took place between two people.
6. Forgive yourself for any negative thoughts, emotions or feelings that you have had about others, yourself or events. In some cases, it may help to forgive oneself first before forgiving others. You should not

use this as an opportunity to relive the incident but see it purely as what it really was, an incident of life in which one person violated another with little thought of the other person's feelings (for they are always there).

7. Allow any negative emotions that have been associated with the incident to be cleared or dispersed. This may include sadness, grief and feeling of loss. The important thing is to be gentle with yourself and not beat yourself up over this incident or the feelings it has created within you. It is also good to acknowledge and appreciate that you are human and that it's very likely that there are other incidents from your past that you wish to forgive as well (there may be several at once, which makes it tricky).

8. Be open to receiving any healing energies or love which have been directed at your situation during this period of quiet reflection. It is believed that you may receive counseling, forgiveness, guidance and the power of attraction during this time. It is important to remember that everything happens with a purpose and so there must be some reason you are encountering these situations at this time on your journey. You may also wish to ask God or the Universe to help you heal from this situation or accept the forgiveness of others involved in it.

9. Once you have finished your Ho'oponopono mediation, it may help to discuss what happened with someone close to you after it has finished, particularly if something significant occurred during this time.

Conclusion

After reading the book, you now understand what mindfulness and meditation are and how to use them in your everyday life. You can even sit on a bus and focus solely on your breath since mindfulness is so beautiful and simple to practice. Even at work, you are able to meditate for a short period of time during lunch. You'll feel refreshed and able to focus on your work as a result. There are many facets to this beautiful practice. Many different meditation techniques are available, and they have assisted even seasoned criminals in shedding their criminality and reverting to lawfulness. The notorious inmates in India's jails sobbed as Sri Sri Ravi Shankar, a well-known spiritual leader and founder of the Art of Living Foundation, led a meditation session there. Such is meditation's power.

Well-known sages, masters, and gurus have been engaging in and passing down this great practice for the past 5000 years. The practice of meditation demonstrates how to have a happy, joyful, and contented existence. The most fundamental aspect of our existence is the freedom to think, speak, and live, and meditation aids us in doing just that.

It's been said that mastering meditation involves mastering release. Giving up the wheel and allowing oneself to experience stillness is an act of surrender. Our innate desire is for control, and we constantly want to move on to new things. Because we try to juggle all those balls at once, our frenzied thought processes lead us to assume that we are skilled at multi-tasking. As a result, our lives start to resemble the hamster's busy wheel-racing existence.

We have the chance to pause, calm our brains, and establish a secure space where we may actually start to know ourselves through meditation. So, be ready to let go of the reins and immerse yourself in the silence, whether you start your trip in search of health, stress alleviation, or spiritual knowledge. You will leave this area feeling energized, enlightened, and empowered. This is your haven of tranquility.

To manage stress, recover physically and mentally, discover more serenity and harmony in your life, increase your productivity at work or in sports, or just to be a nicer person, you might start meditating. Regular meditation makes all of these things possible. Therefore it makes sense to start your meditation practice with one of these goals in mind. But meditation introduces us to our innermost essence, the truth of who we truly are, making it the best present you can give to yourself or if you can, a loved one. You ask yourself, "Who am I?" and then you search within. You learn the answers to problems that have troubled you for a while. Finally, you experience a complete cycle.

When practicing mindfulness, you must focus on each individual bodily part. You become conscious of yourself by doing this. After concentrating on each area of your body, such as your right leg, right knee, right hand, fingers, right eye, and right ear, switch to your left side. Now that your eyes are open concentrate on just one thing in the space. It might be anything, like a pen stand or a vase for flowers. Spend a minute trying to concentrate on it, then look away. Keep your attention on your breathing and your body parts as you do this. You become conscious of your environment, your breathing, and yourself thanks to this threefold attention. You can follow along with this using an audio CD.

By mentally inhaling deeply during meditation, we are able to return to the present moment with renewed vigor and greater power to meet the problems of daily life. Even while meditation is a lifestyle, most people may easily incorporate it into their everyday routines without needing to make significant changes to their lives.

Meditation doesn't call for specialized equipment, pricey memberships, regular meetings, or dietary restrictions like other fitness programs do. You get to choose the location, the timing, and even the duration that best suits your way of life. How this program functions for you is entirely up to you. It doesn't matter your age or level of fitness; meditation is for you. It is also completely nonreligious. There is definitely no justification for delaying the commencement of this procedure and receiving the rewards, which will only enhance your life both now and in the future.

Printed in Great Britain
by Amazon